GG

Cleans House

Learning Teamwork

RENEE GOODWIN

CITIOFBOOKS, INC.
3736 Eubank NE Suite A1
Albuquerque, NM 87111-3579
www.citiofbooks.com

Published by Citi of Books 2025

ISBN   979-8-89391-500-6   (paperback)
ISBN   979-8-89391-499-3   (hardcover)
ISBN   979-8-89391-501-3   (ebook)

Library of Congress Control Number 2025902295

Printed in the United States of America

Acknowledgments

I am thankful for my heavenly guidance for inspiring me to take "My leap of Faith."

I am thankful to my children for introducing me to the Cane Corso Breed (Italian Mastiff) and helping our family find Leonidas Maximus "Leo" and Gorgo Cecilia "GG."

To my dear family and friends, thank you for your excitement for this achievement. It truly means the world to me.

I would like to extend special thanks to the Citi of Books team of experts for their enthusiasm and encouragement through our publishing journey.

To Gabriela Fleming, thank you for your tremendous graphic design work.

I send a warm thank you to Donna Cummings Photography for a memorable photo shoot and fantastic photos.

1

Hi. My name is Gorgo Cecilia, but everyone calls me GG. I have a happy home with My Mr. and Mrs. Gee. They love me and care for me.

I have great news to share. My Mrs. Gee told me that today my friend Susie, the housekeeper, is coming. My Mrs. Gee, Susie, and I clean the house together. We call this *teamwork*.

My Mrs. Gee always starts with the laundry. So I help her carry the clothes. Socks are the most fun to carry. I can run down the hall and race My Mrs. Gee to the laundry room. My Mrs. Gee smiles and says, "GG, you are so funny!"

Susie likes to make the bed first. I admit I would rather stay curled up and take a nap, but once the action starts, I am all in. I help change the sheets and pillowcases. Susie laughs and says, "GG, you are so funny!"

Next, it is my turn. I like to clean the shower. I help spread the water all around by shaking all over. Water goes everywhere. It is great. My Mrs. Gee and Susie both giggle and say, "GG, you are so funny!"

We all help clean the kitchen. I help My Mrs. Gee load the dishwasher. My Mrs. Gee puts the dishes in, and I give them a quick lick. I call this "prewashing." My Mrs. Gee just smiles and says, "GG, you are so funny!"

As Susie wipes the table, I am on "crumb duty." I wait for crumbs to fall so I can help clean the floor. Susie laughs and says, "GG, you are so funny!"

Now the time arrives for the most fun of all. It is what My Mrs. Gee calls vacuuming. I call it "Let the Race Begin." My Mrs. Gee flips the switch and *vroooom*. I start running around, trying to keep up so I can help clean the carpet. My Mrs. Gee goes left, then right, and turns around. So I go right, then left, and about face. She goes faster and faster. So I go faster and faster.

17

Finally, out of breath, My Mrs. Gee says, "GG, you are so funny. You win."

Oh, I am excited to hear those words because that means it is time for a treat. I just love *teamwork*. *Teamwork* is so rewarding.

Vocabulary Word

Teamwork – join together to help.

About the Author

Renee Goodwin, award-winning author of GG Life Lesson Storybook Series ® children's books has an undying passion for education. She learned early in her life, the importance of education witnessing her parents working several jobs during the day then attending school at night to better support their family.

Renee received her upper-level education at Texas A&M University in College Station, Texas graduating with an undergraduate Bachelor of Science degree in curriculum and instruction (mathematics and chemistry). She was a teacher in the Bryan/College Station area and at St. Gregory Cathedral School and Bishop Thomas K. Gorman Catholic High School in Tyler, Texas.

Renee earned an undergraduate Bachelor of Science degree in petroleum engineering from Texas A&M University and is a registered professional engineer in the State of Texas. Renee earned a Master of Business Administration degree from the University of Texas at Tyler.

She was the first woman offshore drilling engineer supervisor in the Gulf of Mexico for British Petroleum. She established an oil and gas corporation, TP Exploration Inc. based in Tyler, Texas, and served as President/CEO for thirty years.

Renee is the recipient of the 2021 Texas A&M University, Aggie Women Legacy Award. She is honored that her GG Life Lesson Storybook Series ® books are exhibited in the Children's Collection of the Texas A&M University Cushing Library and in the Robert R. Muntz Library at the University of Texas at Tyler.

Renee is thrilled for her GG Life Lesson Storybook, *GG Cleans House – Learning Teamwork* to be showcased at prominent book fairs across the United States and Internationally and featured in the 2025/2026 New York Times Book Review. She is a 2025 Marquis Who's Who Biographical Listee.

Renee has continued her family educational legacy providing a sound intellectual foundation for her sons who have earned their undergraduate degrees and master's degrees leading them to their established careers.

Renee recognizes the value of creating an appreciation for ones' education. With her GG Life Lesson Storybook Series ® children's books, she hopes to share her endless enthusiasm for learning.

Renee enjoys creating acrylic artworks, cooking, horseback riding, playing the guitar and line dancing exercise. She is always delighted to volunteer for school, church and community events.

Renee resides in Tyler, Texas where she shares precious moments with her husband, family, and friends, with Leo, GG's best friend, and her always entertaining, deeply inspirational, and forever beloved GG. You can read more about the author, GG and friends and order personally autographed GG Life Lesson Storybook Series ® books for your family and friends on Renee's websites (www.ggstorybooks.com) and (www.goodwinglobalpublishing.com).

www.ingramcontent.com/pod-product-compliance
Lightning Source LLC
Chambersburg PA
CBRC090805300326
41914CB00069B/1643